WITHDRAWN

RECENT DEVELOPMENTS
IN ROMAN CATHOLIC THOUGHT

PATHWAY BOOKS

A SERIES OF CONTEMPORARY EVANGELICAL STUDIES

BIOGRAPHICAL NOTE

GERRIT CORNELIS BERKOUWER is Professor of Systematic Theology at the Free University of Amsterdam, The Netherlands. From this position he has been busily engaged in teaching both continental and American students of theology and in contributing to contemporary theological discussion. In the United States he is best known for his *Studies in Dogmatics,* six volumes of which have already appeared, and for his articles in *Christianity Today.*

He is also the author of an important work on Roman Catholicism, *The Conflict with Rome,* and of a penetrating study of Karl Barth's theology, *The Triumph of Grace in the Theology of Karl Barth.*

Recent Developments in Roman Catholic Thought

by

G. C. BERKOUWER

Professor of Systematic Theology
in the Free University,
Amsterdam, The Netherlands

WM. B. EERDMANS PUBLISHING COMPANY

L.C. catalog card number, 58-9543

Printed in the United States of America

First printing, May 1958

*Translated from the Dutch
by J. J. LAMBERTS,
Assistant Professor of English,
Northwestern University*

CONTENTS

INTRODUCTION

DOES IT make any sense to speak about the *development* of Roman Catholic thought? Does not Rome, after all, always remain the same, unsubjected to actual changes in the course of history? Is not Rome the *Roma æterna,* the unchangeable Rome, and are not all apparent changes resolved within its unchangeability?

It is not easy to give an answer to these questions. One can speak about changeability as well as unchangeability. On the one hand there is a historical development of the church, its institutions, and its dogma; there is a process of growth in the course of centuries. At the same time the continuity is extremely strong. And this continuity is not there by accident. It is directly associated with the Roman Catholic idea of the Church of Christ — the single reality of the body of Christ upon earth with doctrinal authority which under the direct presence of the Spirit is endowed with an infallible character. And it is particularly with respect to the infallibility of this doctrinal authority that the question arises from time to time whether it is possible to speak of actual changes within the Roman Catholic Church.

When we undertake a discussion of contemporary developments in Roman Catholicism, we certainly cannot afford to lose sight of this continuity. In the nineteenth century Modernism tried to bring about an actual change with regard to parts of the doctrine of the Roman Cath-

olic Church, but this Modernism was ceremoniously rejected. The unchangeability of the Roman church had
been severely challenged, but the church maintained the
great fundamental lines of its existence. In our considerations therefore we shall be able to speak about change
only if we see it in direct relationship to the unchangeability, which is, as it were, symbolized in the single,
papal authority in Rome.

It does, however, make sense to speak about changes,
because it is precisely these changes which illuminate the
unchangeability.

The Roman Catholic Church really desires change, pro-
gression, recognition of the development of learning. It
does not want conservatism, but wishes to stand in the
midst of modern scholarship. Over against many attempts in the past to forbid any contact with learning as
being dangerous, the Roman Catholic Church in our
time operates in intimate association with contemporary
learning and culture. And the great question in present-
day Catholicism is whether this association is possible without jeopardizing the unchangeability of the church.

We see this particularly in connection with recent Roman Catholic Biblical research. It is true that Rome, as
was determined in the sixteenth century at the Council
of Trent, accepts tradition as a source of revelation of
equal value with Holy Scripture, but it likewise accepts
Holy Scripture as infallible. Because Biblical research has
gained status in recent Roman Catholic thought, the question naturally arises whether from out of the Word of
God a power might not come by which the unchangeability of Rome would become relative.

As far as Rome itself is concerned, this is once and for all excluded. Rome believes that it is impossible for conflicts to exist between the Bible and the established teaching of the church. Both spring from the same source and they do not come into conflict. Modern Biblical scholarship, according to Rome, can do nothing except support and establish the doctrine of the church.

When, however, we take up contemporary developments in Roman Catholic thought, we do so because precisely in the relationship between developments and continuity questions arise which are important, and the Reformation church and theology must pay full attention to them. These questions are important because the relationship between Rome and the Reformation continues to keep us occupied. The Reformation is such an impressive breach in the history of the Church (second to that between the Eastern and Western church in 1054) that it does not leave us in peace. And when we really accept the Reformation we do well to become acquainted with Roman Catholicism in all its unchangeability and in its shifts and changes during the course of history. In this short study we wish first to observe where the unchangeability of the Roman church appears, and then against this background to examine to what extent we may speak of changes and shifts.

Whenever we thus occupy ourselves with the Roman Catholic Church we must keep in mind that we may not adopt a negative attitude, a barren anti-papism. The note of *anti* is sounded in the Reformation, but this *anti* is positive, not negative. Every kind of Protestantism that stands merely in a protest-relationship is stricken with un-fruitfulness.

That is why the name *Reformation* signifies far more than Protestantism. There have been many protests during the centuries. There are even forms of Protestantism which have let go of the gospel in its true sense and which see no more in Protestantism than a protest against doctrinal authority, absolutism, and heteronomy. We have in mind here the principal weakness of liberal Protestantism, which is really no longer thriving on the power of the Reformation but which in fact has broken with the Reformation and combats Roman Catholicism from a modernistic Protestant standpoint. The positive thesis of the Reformation is absent from this protest. The drama in the evolution of Protestantism is that the *anti,* the protest, is not always apparent. Every protest against the Roman Catholic Church must be based upon the gospel, the Word of God, which only is capable of resisting the assumption of the Roman Catholic Church that it is the only and true Church of Christ.

Nor may the struggle of the Reformation faith arise from anxiety; it must arise from the conviction that the question is the reformation of the Church, the true authority of the gospel, the Church in its wrestling, and the bringing of the gospel into the world. Only from the truth in the Reformation will it be possible to serve the Church and also the world with the gospel of the grace of God, which is a power of God unto salvation. It is in this frame of mind that we wish to occupy ourselves with Roman Catholicism in our time.

CHAPTER ONE

EX CATHEDRA — THE GREAT FASCINATION

———————

IN A TIME of irresolution, when uncertainty oppresses the heart, many people are very fascinated by words of absolute certainty. This explains why today many people are once more ready to pay attention whenever they hear the trumpet-call of certainty.

Of course one must not generalize at this point. There are also those who become thoroughly annoyed by expressions of certainty because these expressions seem to be carried over from a bygone era when unshaken certainties could still be commended. Anyone who has been seized by irrationalism feels himself insulted by "certainties"; he finds them intolerable, for they accuse him of his own uncertainty. Moreover, the expression "we know" strikes many as a piece of insufferable arrogance. This explains why the Church is frequently accused of pretending to know everything. No one else knows anything, but the Church "knows" everything — so its critics charge — and confidently proceeds on its way, serene in the face of the misery of shaken certainties and the barrenness of life.

But it remains a fact that in the uncertainty of our times the call of certainty fascinates many hearts, particularly when this certainty is loudly acclaimed as an escape from the general desolation, as a shining light in the darkness.

This is why it is very important that we know from what direction and in what manner the assurance of un-assailability comes. Is it a responsible assurance? In the realm of politics we often hear daring utterances in times of crisis which cause the inspiration of the people to return and which awaken the hope that life has meaning. Thus we sometimes find courage reviving in the midst of bleak times.

From this it is quite clear that the declaration of an infallible certainty always evokes the question of standards. Is the origin of the proclaimed certainty a legitimate one, or are its sources to be found in the obscure recesses of the human heart? That question is of extraordinary concern in each era. In the church's struggle, too, the question of standards is important. It is a fact not to be ignored that there still remains a voice which resounds through the world and which in diametrical opposition to other voices proclaims a final certainty. It is the voice of the church, which is joined in the radical struggle concerning the character of certainty. Here we meet the certainty of the Roman Catholic *ex cathedra,* the infallible expression of the head of the Roman church.

Frequently this infallible utterance is commended as the solution to the misery of uncertainty and as an invitation to peoples and individuals to return to the fountainhead of stability and calm. It is understandable that there are people who respond, and that now this one and now that one pursues the path which promises such a certain future. For there is no question more urgent

than the question of certainty. It concerns everyone and
it touches the most profound problems of life. It is not
an abstract question in theology, but a question which
every human being encounters in one way or another, and
one which clamors for solution. There has never been a
person who was happy about his uncertainty. And when
a voice is heard which speaks with great positiveness, there
are always people who pay attention. This was already
a critical problem many centuries ago when the false
prophets opposed God's prophets and their "thus saith
the Lord," and the public was confronted with the dilemma of two "certainties." During the first centuries of the
Christian Church, too, certainty was preached which con-
flicted head-on with Christian certainty. And the question of certainty remains a burning one. Above the
clamor of many diverse voices we can distinguish the call
of Rome: *ex cathedra.*

*   *   *

The oft-posed question regarding the real meaning of
ex cathedra is not so difficult to answer. Whenever Rome
speaks of papal infallibility it means least of all a personal quality of the pope, or a general infallibility in his
personal life. It means, rather, an attribute ascribed to
the pope as the head of the church when he makes utterances regarding matters of faith and morals which concern the entire church. It is an imparted attribute which
depends on the assistance of the Holy Spirit. This certainty thus has a solid foundation, so that it can become
a word for every age. All doubt can be resolved in the
dazzling light of this unassailability.

A more difficult question to answer is: Which expressions of papal authority are to be distinguished as *ex-cathedra?* In the year 1302 a bull was promulgated regarding the relationship between church and state. It has often been asked whether this, too, was an infallible expression on the matter of the doctrine of the two swords, for it is obvious that this doctrine is not universally accepted. There are prominent theologians who no longer accept the doctrine that the temporal and the spiritual sword are at the disposal of the church. They maintain, rather, that the one is wielded by the church and the other by the state (at the bidding of the priest and as long as he approves). It has been publicly stated, "This doctrine is not correct and is at present accepted by no one." Hence one must be careful about designating utterances as *ex cathedra.* According to Roman Catholic writers such utterances are relatively infrequent. Nor is it always specifically stated when an utterance is *ex cathedra,* the result being that all kinds of uncertainty may arise later on. There is certainly no doubt that the proclamation regarding the assumption of Mary (1950) took place *ex cathedra,* and there does not appear to be any discussion about it.

Regardless of how difficult this doctrine may seem, nevertheless the light of its "certainty" beams over the world, at the same time suggestive and menacing. It is a warning against rationalists and irrationalists; it is a comfort to doubting spirits who have lost their certainty. Everything else can be subjected to discussion but not this certainty. It stands above the valleys of doubt, elevated in a divine and protective light, like the pillar of cloud which was darkness to the enemies but light for the children of Israel.

We have become accustomed to speak casually about the pretensions of infallibility, but we must not forget that each uncertainty of Protestantism and each discussion about "ultimate truth" prepares hearts for this call of certainty. Our own position is challenged each time such a claim resounds. There are always people who are weary of their uncertainty and who at length no longer care to raise the question of standards. Finally, they give themselves up to this certainty which is not subject to standards. Who would not like to be rid of the struggle and the debate, and who does not long for the final word?

This weariness is a danger for the human heart. It was Augustine who said: Our spirits long for rest until they find rest in God. But one may also seek for rest where the voice of certainty is heard above the struggle and hesitation. Then problems which existed previously seem to fall away; they are removed by this inextinguishable light. Cares seem to be taken away by an authority which stands higher than all quarrels.

This is the danger of the fascinating call of certainty *ex cathedra* in a time when people have become estranged from the gospel and when uncertainty occupies their hearts. One may surrender without first thoroughly examining the offered certainty. I do not say that this kind of surrender is universal: who is able to penetrate into the final deliberations of the heart? But there is a great danger that uncertain times lead the way to certainties in which the question of standards is no longer raised because it appears to have been resolved once and for all in this *ex cathedra*.

Over against this *ex cathedra* certainty the Reformation subjected all of life to the Word, not only the individual person, but the entire Church in all its operations; and as a result it accorded high honor to the glorious rule of Jesus Christ. One must not say that the Reformation teaching creates a tension which cannot be endured, and that one had better "know with certainty" than to follow the way of the Reformers. For the meaning of this rule is precisely that it leads men to unassailable certainty. This certainty, however, is one in which the self-sufficiency of man is radically crushed, and in which his entire certainty is founded on a subjection to the Word of God. Christ's rule has meaning for the utmost reaches of the Church, and extends over all of man's life. Its concern, however, is not with personal matters and peculiarities but with the ultimate question of certainty.

In times when many people are skeptical about the very word "certain" the question should be asked whether one can merely stand by the side of the road, rationally or irrationally, or whether one who so stands is not already involved in life — in certainties and uncertainties. If anything has become clear as the result of the struggle of the ages it is this, that one can say: Tell me what your certainties are, and I will tell you what kind of person you are; I will tell you how you make your pathway through life, and how you will build that life in the future.

Whoever rejects the *ex cathedra* may know that he does not necessarily surrender his life to the fearfulness of uncertainty. Fortunately there is no reason why a dilemma should exist between *ex cathedra* and tormenting skepticism. To the followers of the Reformation is given the task of pointing the way with the witness of their life.

CHAPTER TWO

INFALLIBLE DECISIONS

―――――――

ANYONE WHO reflects upon the unchangeability of the Roman Catholic Church and at the same time keeps in mind the developments of the past one hundred years is particularly impressed by two decisive events, namely, the proclamation of the infallibility of the Pope in 1870 at the Vatican Council, and the pronouncement by the Roman Catholic Church regarding Mary. It is difficult to determine which of the events has greater significance. Each bears evidence of the conscious advance of the Roman Catholic Church; each is the conclusion of a development that has been going on for centuries, thereby accentuating the unchangeability of the church.

In the first place, let us examine the infallibility of the Pope. It has frequently been said that this decision occurred late in church history. We do not care to go into this now, but we do wish to point out that although the decision occurred in 1870, a long development preceded it, and that the decision simply expressed something that had long been alive in the church. Of tremendous significance in this development was the Council of Trent in the sixteenth century. At this Council the Reformation was rejected and therewith the Biblical principle of *sola Scriptura*. This does not mean that the Council of

Trent failed to accept the infallibility of the Bible. It announced that all of Scripture is to be regarded as the infallible Word of God. But in opposition to the Reformation, which appealed to Scripture against the deformation of the Roman Catholic Church, the Council of Trent proclaimed that there are two sources of revelation which must be accepted with equal reverence: Scripture and tradition. It defended the proposition that these two sources are of equal value, and maintained that the criticism of the Reformation was without force when it asked: Where are we taught this in Scripture? For if Scripture and tradition have equal status, then one cannot appeal to Scriptures alone.

After Trent the power of tradition continued to grow stronger, while as early as 1564 (directly following the Council of Trent) the Pope came to be regarded as the person who had the right to interpret and to establish tradition.

We are here brought face to face with an obvious development. Whenever another source of knowledge is placed alongside Scripture as being of equal value, we observe that eventually Scripture becomes relegated to the background. Whenever people place reason next to the Bible, or emotion, then ultimately one source supplants the other and causes it gradually to fade away. Then we get either rationalism or mysticism. It is true, Scripture is not simply pushed to the side, but it is, as it were, in captivity. Since the Council of Trent tradition has advanced further and further into the foreground.

By this same process there eventually came about the decision of the Vatican Council in 1870, when the infal-

libility of the Pope was promulgated. Holy Scripture
was not rejected then either. It continued to be maintained as a source of revelation just as it had been at
Trent, but it could not officiate, it could not unfold its
power. The shadow of a competitor had fallen across
its place in the church.

Although the Vatican Council emphatically declared
that the Pope as a person is not infallible and that he
is infallible only when he speaks as head of the church,
ex cathedra, and when he speaks in matters of faith and
morals, and although it declared that the doctrine does
not involve revelation (*new* revelation) or inspiration by
the Holy Spirit (as in the case of Holy Scripture), it did
profess an infallibility which is founded upon the so-
called *assistentia divina,* the divine presence of the Holy
Spirit. Through this presence the church is safeguarded
against all error. No one need have any doubts about the
establishment of a dogma, nor may one have such doubts.
This infallibility is the fulfillment of the Savior's promise
to the Church, that the Spirit would lead it into all truth.
Thus once again we are confronted by the unchangeability
of the Roman church!

It is necessary to add that in an infallible utterance
regarding doctrine the Pope does not proclaim a *new*
dogma. Spokesmen for the Roman Catholic Church are
emphatic in stating that there cannot be a new dogma.
The guidance of the Holy Spirit does not produce a new
dogma; rather it enables the Pope to establish that what
is now proclaimed belongs, and did belong, to the original treasury of revelation. This treasury of revelation
was closed at the death of the last of the apostles, and
thus there is no *new* dogma. That a particular dogma

did form a part of this treasury — this is what the Pope proclaims, and in his infallibility he lays before the entire church the irrefutable certainty that the light now shining so brilliantly is in truth the light of divine revelation.

One can, it is true, compare this dogma with Holy Scripture, but the comparison may not be done out of fear that the two are possibly in conflict. Conflict is ruled out a priori. Harmony is established from the beginning. All doubt is condemned and rejection is declared heresy.

Thus the decision of 1870 strongly accentuated the unchangeability of the church. Who can resist the will of God? And the Roman church declared with emphasis that in its voice resounds the voice of the Shepherd of the Church and that blessed is he who finds no offense in Him.

* * *

Now the decision of 1870 is, to be sure, not the only one during the past century which has been of importance. Equally noteworthy are the two closely related proclamations regarding Mary. These, too, have had a long development. Already at the Council of Trent — although there was still no independent dogma about Mary — an exception regarding Mary was made in the decree regarding original sin. The development eventually led to the decision of 1854, when the immaculate conception of Mary was proclaimed. Since that year Mariology has continued to increase in the Roman Catholic Church. Without exaggeration we may say that we are witnessing the Mary-phase of Catholicism.

In 1858 Mary appeared, so it is maintained, at Lourdes to Bernadette Soubirous, a fourteen-year-old girl. In this appearance, so the story goes, Mary replied in answer to a question about her identity: "I am the immaculate conception." From then on the name Lourdes has re sounded over the entire world. Millions of pilgrims journey to this holy place where the wonders of God by means of the mysterious fountain are said to constitute an irrefutable witness to the dogma of 1854.

As early as 1870 there was general agreement with respect to the bodily assumption of Mary, but because the Vatican Council of that year was prematurely adjourned, this dogma did not then become established. It did, however, continue to evolve. In 1943 Pope Pius XII, in a postscript to a famous encyclical, proclaimed that the most holy mother is honored of God in heaven in body and soul. And in 1950 the church proclaimed that the bodily assumption of Mary belonged to the original treasury of revelation of the Church — the conclusion, for the time being, of the Mariological development.

*   *   *

The well-known television speaker Monsignor Fulton J. Sheen once made the remark that it was not entirely a matter of chance that VJ-day and the Feast of the Assumption of Mary both happened to fall on the 15th of August, and that from this it was evident that Mary had delivered victory to America. In response to this, Martin Rist, professor of New Testament Theology in Denver, asked ironically what Mary had been doing on the dark day of Pearl Harbor. One may regard this as a somewhat unkind comment, but here we come to a profound prob lem, namely, a Mariological appeal to the providence of

God. I do not imagine that Fulton Sheen was particularly impressed by Rist's criticism. He undoubtedly regarded it as a failure to appreciate the Divine and Mariological intervention in world history.

Rist also cited an account from a book by Upton Sinclair in which the author transports Mary to Los Angeles. This Jewish girl is so alarmed by the honor accorded her person that she begs to be returned to the rusticity of Galilee. No doubt neither Sinclair nor Rist thought that they could explode a long, long tradition with suggestions like these.

Before the official proclamation it was quite apparent that for a long time the members of the church had run ahead of the teachers of the church with respect to the doctrine of Mary's assumption (Assumption Day has been the most popular of the Mary holidays). Commenting on this a Roman Catholic writer once called to mind Peter and John: John ran faster than Peter and reached the sepulchre before him. At the time of the proclamation mention was made in a Roman Catholic periodical of a voice that was inspired (contrary to the teachings of the Council of 1870). But even though the voice was not inspired, the dogma is still considered, in accord with the Council, the fruit of the presence of the Holy Spirit. Ave Maria . . . .

In 1948 Bishop Terrier of Bayonne, on the occasion of a Marian crusade, directed a letter to a hundred missionaries. He recalled that in answer to Nietzsche's "God is dead," the echo responded, "Man is dead." But then he turns his attention to Mary: "To find her in her immaculateness, in her tranquility, is not this truly to find man, the Paradise-creature, as the Creator wished it?"

And when Pope Pius XII established the dogma in 1950, he announced in his encyclical that we, in this time of dehumanization, can see once more, in Mary, how much a human life is worth when it is completely dedicated to the will of the Father. In a time — according to the encyclical — in which the doctrine of materialism and the corruption of morality arising from it threaten to overwhelm virtue and to annihilate mankind by new wars, it is now made completely clear for what glory our body and soul have been destined.

Thus the Pope endeavors to clarify the meaning of the Mariological dogma. It is a protest against dehumanization and against existentialism's devaluation of human life. He seeks to point out that destiny of mankind which is manifested in the glorification of the mother of God. Apparently the worth of man has not been sufficiently revealed in the resurrection and ascension of Jesus Christ; now it must be made clear in Mary. The grim forces of dehumanization are met by her example, by this human being who has cooperated in the work of salvation. Immaculate humanity . . . .

*   *   *

One of the most important questions raised by Protestantism following this decision has been whether the Pope can find support in Holy Scripture for this dogma. It is, after all, quite obvious that the Bible has nothing to say about the assumption of Mary. The last mention of Mary occurs in Acts 1 where she (not named until after the disciples), along with the others, is waiting for the coming of the Spirit. Would the Pope yet endeavor to point out a basis in Scripture, particularly since the tradition of the first six centuries is not strong — a judgment which even Roman Catholic theologians make?

It is quite clear that in Roman Catholic theology the assumption is not based on passages from the Bible, but on Mary's being full of grace, on her being free from the curse, "Dust thou art and to dust shalt thou return." The dogma is part of the total Mary-picture and is intimately related to the idea that Christ and Mary are inseparable.

How does the encyclical express itself regarding this dogma? The official proclamation, *ex cathedra* without a shadow of doubt, says:

> The immaculate, forever virgin, mother of God, Mary, after she had completed her earthly life, was taken up with body and soul into heavenly glory.

Thus states the proclamation of "Bishop Pius, servant of the servants of God by the authority of our Lord Jesus Christ, and of the blessed apostles Peter and Paul, and of us." The warning is added that anyone who may henceforth doubt or deny this doctrine is utterly fallen away from the divine and catholic faith.

In the encyclical an attempt is made to base this dogma upon Sacred Scripture. All kinds of texts are cited to which, according to the encyclical, the fathers have referred, as for example, Psalm 132:8: "Arise, O Lord, into thy rest; thou, and the ark of thy strength," the ark being the image of Mary; Psalm 45:9ff: "Upon thy right hand did stand the queen in gold of Ophir"; Song of Solomon

3:6: "Who is this that cometh out of the wilderness like pillars of smoke, perfumed with myrrh and frankincense, with all the powders of the merchant?" Revelation 12:1: "A woman clothed with the sun."

The Pope, however, gives no official exegesis of these Scriptures in support of the dogma. That, it may be said, would be possible. When a Frenchman referred to such texts in this connection, another Roman Catholic dogmatist asserted that his evidence was so feeble that refutation was unnecessary.

But the encyclical of 1950 placidly quotes these texts as though since the Middle Ages no satisfactory exegesis of them has been given. And while the encyclical does not give an exegesis, it conjoins them with the dogma as though the Church Fathers used them in this way. Thus it gives simply the illusion of Biblical evidence. In reality the Holy Scripture plays no part.

The dogma is simply the climax of a Mariological evolution: Mary triumphing with Christ. The road is open for further dogma to follow. The discussion is now under way, not regarding the dispensation of grace by Mary (this is already a doctrine of the church), but regarding redemption by Mary: Mary as co-redeemer, a co-savior with Christ.

*   *   *

The Roman Catholic proclamations of the last one hundred years regarding infallibility and regarding Mary are so clear and so positive that it hardly seems possible still to speak about "recent developments in Roman Catholic thought." Is there more to be said about Rome than simply that it is unchangeable?

CHAPTER THREE

THE NEW APPRAISAL OF LUTHER

IN OBSERVING the newer currents in Roman Catholicism, we should first of all note its recent evaluation of the Reformation and particularly Martin Luther. In the past this judgment was fierce and lacerating. A book could be written about the annihilating judgments passed upon the Reformers, upon Luther and Calvin, in which an effort was made to account for their work of reformation by means of a moral defect in their lives. Fantastic stories were told about their lives and their deaths. Writers have pointed to Luther's pride and anarchy, to his sinful nature which induced him at an evil hour to lay his own difficulties to the charge of the church.

Now it is well to bear in mind that these judgments were not merely the personal estimates of Luther. Rome itself, until the present century, frequently shared them. We are reminded here of the notorious Borromeo encyclical issued in 1910 on the occasion of the tercentenary of Carlo Borromeo's canonization. Borromeo lived from 1538 to 1584 and was a fiery defender of the Roman Catholic Church. What did he fight against? Listen to the answer of the encyclical:

> . . . [There] rose up proud and rebellious men, *enemies of the cross of Christ* . . . . men of *earthly*

sentiments whose god is their belly (Philippians 3:18, 19). These, bent not on correcting morals but on denying the dogmas, multiplied disorders, loosening for themselves and for others the bridle of licentiousness, and contemning the authoritative guidance of the Church to pander to the passions of the most corrupt princes and peoples, with a virtual tyranny overturned its doctrine, constitution, discipline.

Then, imitating these sinners to whom was addressed the menace: *Woe to you who call evil good and good evil* (Isaiah 5:20), that tumult of rebellion and that perversion of faith and morals they called reformation and themselves reformers. But, in truth, they were corrupters . . . .

So much for the encyclical of 1910. In it there arises an image of the Reformation which presents a multitude of deceivers being divinely confronted by the true restorers, among whom is Borromeo.

When in 1910 there arose protests against this encyclical from every direction, someone undertook to defend the encyclical and wrote that everything was quite clear if one simply looked at the difference between Borromeo and Luther. Borromeo was a man of prayer; Luther despised prayer. Borromeo held Holy Scripture in honor; Luther falsified Scripture.

We do not want to discuss this grim encyclical any further, for since that time other voices have been raised with regard to Luther. They are the voices of those who seek to explain his appearance by the corruption of the church prior to 1517. These are the men of a conciliatory temperament, who emphasize the darkness of the time before Luther. Moreover, some have written about the

religious motives of Luther and have gone so far as to
show that the Roman Catholic judgment of Luther has
been one-sided, too much influenced by tradition and po-
lemic theology. They have tried to approach the Reformation more historically. Thus in 1943 a Roman
Catholic theologian demonstrated with overwhelming material, that writers had on the whole simply repeated what
Cochlaeus had written against Luther in a book dated
1549, a very influential book which went through 150
printings. This same Catholic writer mentioned that the
atmosphere had been poisoned and that it was necessary
to break with this spell. And so there is now a far
sharper accent upon Luther's religious motives.

There is, for instance, the conciliator Yves Congar, who
sees quite different things in Luther than his Catholic
predecessors saw, and he is disturbed because the protestant movement really was a drama filled with tragedy. Another such critic is Karl Adam, who lays heavy stress upon
the guilt of the Roman church. Here is what he has
written:

> In truth, night had descended over the whole of
> Christendom. This is the conclusion of our obser-
> vations on the end of the fifteenth century: among
> the common people a fearful degeneration of true
> piety to a religious materialism and a sickly hys-
> teria; with the lower and higher clergy a secular
> spirit and a great neglect of duty; and with the su-
> preme shepherds of the church a desire for power
> unworthy of anyone and a sacrilegious abuse of the
> most holy things that were entrusted to them. . . .
> Yes, night had fallen. If Luther has risen then with
> the astonishing gifts of his spirit and heart, his
> brilliant view of the actual elements of Christianity,

his passionate aversion to everything that was not holy and that was not from God, the irresistible force of his religious spirit, his persuasive and fearless word and especially his heroism, with which he matched himself against the powerful ones of those days — if Luther had then employed all these glorious capabilities to extirpate the abuses which cried to high heaven and used them to clear the garden of God of its weeds, and if he had withal remained a faithful member of his church, full of humility and lowliness, upright and pure of heart — then we should still be thankful to him. He would still be our great reformer, the servant of God, dear to us, our minister and shepherd, who could be compared with Thomas Aquinas and Francis of Assisi and not lose his brilliance. Indeed, he would be still greater than they, the greatest saint of the German people, a second Boniface (*Una Sancta: Catholic Unity and Christian Love,* pp. 33, 34).

Of course, Adam does not mean to agree with Luther. Luther still erred when he reared one altar against another, and that is a grave sin. Nevertheless, the image of Luther has been changed.

A similar view of Luther is taken by Joseph Lortz, who wrote a book about the Reformation in Germany. Lortz appreciates the fact that in opposition to Scholasticism Luther went back once again to the riches of the New Testament. There his strength lay, and in this return is the explanation of his powerful influence. Powerful, too, was the force of his religious feeling, of his prayer, of his oratory. Luther, according to this author, had no wrong intentions, and anyone who reads Luther's book, *Regarding the Freedom of a Christian,* sees what salutary effects Luther's concepts might have had within the church.

Calvin also shares in this appraisal. It has been said of him that he was saturated with the glory of God. Thus in general we may say that Catholic authors now seek to do justice to the religious background of the Reformation.

As a matter of fact, the conciliatory voices began to sound so loudly that Pope Pius XII on December 20, 1949, warned against continually drawing attention to the sins of the church especially in presenting an analysis of the Reformation. According to the Pope the apostasy of the Reformation was not getting its just due. The Pope's admonition was particularly directed toward Lortz. Undoubtedly the Pope felt that esteem for the Reformation was gradually becoming too strong and that he could discern in it a danger for the Roman Catholic Church. Ultimately the Pope is not concerned with the good intentions of the Reformers, but with an event, a historic event and its consequences. And he points back to that which finally all Roman Catholics accept: the church's historic judgment upon the Reformation, namely, the Reformation was a revolution within the church. Congar, Adam, and Lortz are willing to subscribe to this too.

It is true, however, that the spirit of the Borromeo encyclical is no longer there. The voice has changed. The more people read Luther and Calvin, the more they are impressed by the Reformers' reverence for the Word of God, for their comprehension of the Holy Scriptures, for their love of God. True, they broke with the church, but what a tragedy! Now if they had been immoral peo-

ple (Borromeo encyclical) — but they were indeed religious spirits! The Reformation was a revolution, but
if this voice had echoed within the church . . . .

*   *   *

This conciliatory attitude confronts us with a remarkable situation. While we hear regret expressed over the
fact that the Reformation represented a loss for the
church, since the Reformers broke away, we know that
the Reformation did not break with the church but that,
on the contrary, the church rejected it. As early as 1520,
but especially in 1545, at the Council of Trent, it became
evident that the voice of Reformation was not listened to
or tolerated. Reformation knocked on the door, but the
Council of Trent shut out the *sola fide, sola gratia, sola
scriptura* of the Reformation.

Eventually the men of conciliatory temper will have to
face quite seriously the question, Why did Rome reject
the Reformation? And with this question we come back
to the infallible decisions respecting doctrine. For it is
historically untenable to suppose that the Reformation
wanted a break with the church. In 1517 it had never
occurred to Luther to arouse a revolution. When others
entered upon revolutionary courses, Luther preached
against revolt. With Luther the important matter was
the reformation of the church. But the reformation of
the church invariably arouses opposing forces. This opposition we may see in Rome. All conciliatory voices,
however important, will always evoke the question why
the knock on the door was not answered until our own
time. And the caution of Pope Pius XII gives point to

the question. It is a caution which, as we shall observe later on, turns up once again in an encyclical of 1950.

And yet these conciliatory voices are not unimportant. For they indicate that under the influence of Biblical research there arises a better conception of the Biblical grounds of the Reformation. These grounds are so evident that the Borromeo encyclical does indeed belong to the past.

CHAPTER FOUR

THE NEW THEOLOGY

WHEN WE OBSERVE present-day Roman Catholicism, we especially note the movement which is generally referred to as the New Theology. The new theology has had a number of problems under discussion for more than fifteen years. Its starting-point lies in the school of Lyon-Fourvière, France, with its brilliant representation, of whom the most prominent are : Henri Bouillard, Henri de Lubac Jean Danielou, and Hans Urs von Balthasar. In these men and others we encounter the strong influence of earlier theologians and philosophers, such as Newman, Blondel, and Max Scheler. Our purpose here is not to sketch the historical background, but to indicate what the characteristic features of the theology are.

One of its most prominent features is a concern for the evolution of dogma. According to Rome, this evolution is not in conflict with the infallibility of the doctrinal authority, for during the course of the centuries such a development can be quite clearly traced. Even the decisions of 1870 and 1950, which we have discussed, give evidence that there has been much research in the endeavor to trace the nature of the development of dogma. Back in the nineteenth century Newman (first Anglican and later Roman Catholic) was profoundly occupied with the question of how dogma had resulted from the earlier utterances of the church.

The starting-point of Rome, as we said earlier, is that the treasury of revelation was closed with the death of the last apostle, and that all development must issue from this treasury, under the direction of the ecclesiastical doctrinal authority. Development is the outgrowth of what is already present in the bud. Actually it is not dogma that grows, but knowledge and insight. No new dogma is developed. Rather, the Pope (infallibly) proclaims at a given time in history that this or that dogma belongs, and always has belonged, to the original treasury of revelation. The Vatican Council in 1870 declared that the Holy Spirit was promised to Peter and to his successors not in order that they should learn new truths, but that they by the presence of the Holy Spirit should preserve and explain the substance of the faith. In this way it is possible for material dogma to become formal dogma.

Nevertheless, Roman Catholic theology points to the evolution of dogma as one of the riches of the Church of Rome. It does not regard the course of the church as arbitrary and devious. The course is rather a pure and harmonious unfolding of that which was already present in principle. Roman Catholic theology speaks of the continual development of Catholic truth, which in essence is always and forever the same, but which unfolds itself more fully in the souls of the believers. This evolution, Rome maintains, never touches the substance of dogma. In the course of the centuries nothing of the divine revelation becomes lost. All the pearls of the faith are guarded, but they begin to shine more brightly. There is an emanation from the riches of the truth in accordance with the words of Paul to Timothy: "Keep that which is committed to thy trust" (I Timothy 6:20).

Catholic theologians do not think it at all strange that some important dogmas were not established until the nineteenth and twentieth centuries, for this evolution moves very gradually and in it there is a guidance of the Holy Spirit. Sometimes, as in the Middle Ages, there is opposition to a specific dogma, but then the opposition is little by little overcome. Thus there were, for instance, theologians in the Middle Ages who had difficulties with the immaculate conception of Mary, because they were unable to harmonize this with the universality of original sin. But in the theological consciousness of the church, this doctrine gradually emerged. At the Council of Trent (sixteenth century) no separate Mary-dogma was established, but Mary was made an exception in the decree regarding original sin. We have already noted the powerful developments of the nineteenth and twentieth centuries.

*   *   *

Now it must be observed that Catholic theologians of the New Testament have a special concern for this evolution, and they are not all bent on indicating (like Newman) how purely and harmoniously the development has proceeded. Some are fascinated by the fact that the church and theology always operate with the modes of thought characteristic of the time. They do not point to this process in criticism of the dogma, but they are of the opinion that this process has given a definite coloring not only to the theology but to doctrinal utterances as well.

It is characteristic of the school of new theology that it discovers change occurring in this philosophical shaping. When Henri Bouillard in 1941 wrote a book about Thomas Aquinas he called attention to the philosophical concepts which were maintained in Thomas' time under the influence of the pagan philosopher Aristotle. And he came to the conclusion that it is always possible to speak of an unchanging truth and a changeable formulation, an unchanging content and a changeable form. In other times different forms of philosophical thought gain influence. At one time the forms were Aristotelian, later Hegelian: now some are Heideggerian. And such a process of development is unavoidable. As the church and theology proceed through the centuries they experience the influence of a particular epoch. Philosophical thought is continually changing, and it goes without saying that these changes exert their influence.

Of special importance here is the fact that Bouillard did not make his point with reference only to theology, but he made it also with reference to the infallible doctrinal utterances of the church. For theology, which is after all not infallible, the consequences are not serious. But what about the infallible decisions regarding doctrine, made under the guidance of the Holy Spirit? If it is true that the doctrinal decisions, too, manifest different colorings in relationship to the philosophical forms of thought of a particular time, is it still possible to maintain their infallibility? Does not, at least as regards form, the shadow of changeability fall upon the infallible dogma?

*   *   *

These ideas have caused some Roman Catholic theologians to express concern over the direction of the new theology. Thus, for instance, Garrigou-Lagrange has written that he is convinced that this new theology is on the road to modernism. Already in the nineteenth and early twentieth centuries Rome had had its difficulties with modernism. And this modernism had also been constantly concerned with the development of dogma. It had joined hand in hand with modern scholarship, specifically historical critical research. In 1907 Rome once again sternly rebuked modernism, and in 1910 it proclaimed the anti-modernist oath. In 1908 Alfred Loisy, the French modernist, and George Tyrell, the English modernist, were excommunicated. The modernists had come to an open criticism of the church and its dogma by way of the development of dogma. They saw the Roman Catholic Church standing in a framework of history, and they questioned not only the form of dogma but also its content.

The notable feature of the new theology, however, is that its approach is quite different from the approach of the rejected modernism. There is a point of contact between the two, but the new theology has sought heart and soul to remain Roman Catholic. The new theologians believe that their view regarding the changeable form does not in any manner detract from the unchangeable truth, but that it simply shows that the church has in every period of time actually been in harmony with the forms of thought of that time.

Thus Henri de Lubac lays heavy emphasis on historical dynamics in the development of the church. The church, it is true, rests upon an everlasting foundation, but in every age men are obliged to build their own house. Al-

though truth is objective, we receive truth subjectively;
at various times we do this differently. We are confronted
here with the phenomenon which we may observe in Abra-
ham Kuyper's thought. He wrote that it was necessary
to bring Reformed theology into rapport with human
consciousness in the nineteenth century, and he wanted to
place the treasure of earlier thinking into the molds of
the present. Thus one can speak of old and new Calvinism,
just as Roman Catholics speak of old and New Thomism.
But it is evident that the problem of form and content
becomes particularly acute for the Catholics when it has
to do with the infallible doctrinal declarations of the
church. Can it be possible that along with the form a
certain relativism manages to slip into the content? And
when the church used philosophical forms in its dogma,
how then did the truth fare? There is, for example, the
doctrine of transubstantiation, a doctrine which has an
obvious philosophical structure. If today one thinks
differently regarding the concept of transubstantiation does
not this then have any influence upon the official doctrine
of transubstantiation?

It is evident that these questions encroach deeply on the
whole of Roman Catholic ecclesiastical life. What is one
to think of the fact that this new theology departs quite
sharply from Thomas, while nevertheless in the nineteenth century (1879) Pope Leo XIII published an encyclical (*Aeterni Patris*) in which he commended the great
importance of the philosophical thought of Thomas for all
schools of theology? The Pope observed at the time that

there was development, but precisely into this development he sought to bring the stability necessary to protect
the church from the peril of relativism. The new theology,
however, makes the philosophy of Thomas relative and
endeavors to link it up with modern forms of thought,
for instance, existentialism — naturally not with the atheistic form of existentialism but with existentialism as
viewed by the Roman Catholic existentialist Gabriel Mar-
cel of France. Can all of this be made compatible with
the claim that the Roman Catholic pattern of thought is
unchangeable, or will it become a cause of further conflict? This is the burning question which has been asked
ever since 1940, now here, now there.

*   *   *

A further development in this new theology is a strong
emphasis on the relativity and the limitation of human
knowledge. The new theologians feel that they are not
entirely clear with respect to many problems. Thomas
may have been quite valuable for his time, but now there
are many questions on which clarity cannot be obtained
by an appeal to Thomas. Moreover, the new theologians
wish to stand not on the outside of the development of
knowledge but in the midst of modern problems, without
feeling that there is a distance between church and culture, or between church and science. They do not wish
to be frightened by modern ideas, but rather to consider
them and to incorporate what is of value into the life of
the church. The church may not lag behind, nor may it

forget the intellectuals and ignore the problems which
they raise.

It must be said that the Catholic doctrinal authority
recognizes this. Pope Pius XII is certainly not one to be
averse to knowledge. The question is where to draw the
line. It is possible, following the earlier modernism, to
accept the results of scholarship so uncritically as to
relinquish the Faith. This danger is common to Protes-
tants and Catholics. In Protestantism, too, the problems of
modern scholarship have attained prominence, and here,
too, a synthesis of Christianity and present-day thought
has been attempted. The result has been modernism
and liberalism, with its sharp criticism of, for example,
the church's doctrine of Jesus Christ. Protestant modernism
in the nineteenth century rejected the Chalcedon confession concerning the deity of Christ, and even placed the old
credo — the Apostles' Creed — in jeopardy.

When such events occur there are always people who
become fearful and who toss all scholarship overboard.
They are afraid of it and prefer to turn it over to agnostic
researchers.

There are such timid souls in the Roman Catholic
Church, too, and they are called integralists. After the
modernist oath of 1910 they thought that the Pope should
adopt a far more rigorous course against the dangers of
modernism. But there were others who saw a challenge
in the area of scholarship, for instance, in natural science,
in biology, in the study of Holy Scripture. They did not
want to be afraid, but to pursue their course with caution.
Thus the new theology remained within the orbit of the
church. But the real question was whether the new theology

remained within the bounds of caution. Was dogma not becoming relative? Would these anti-scholastic and anti-speculative currents not lead to an entirely different way of thinking, far removed from the scholastic thought that had set a mark on the church and theology?

To the question what has happened since that time, it may be said that the development has not become modernistic. All of the figures that we named are still members by conviction of the Roman Catholic Church. There have indeed been difficulties. According to Roman Catholic sources, one of the most brilliant exponents of the new theology, Henri de Lubac, was suspended for a time, but he has given new evidence of his faithfulness by writing a study about the mysteries of the church. (This information, however, sounds peculiar because de Lubac never had any misgivings about the mystery of the church. But in any case it is apparent that there have been tensions, although they have not led to a breach.) The adherents of the new theology still constitute the most striking figures in Roman Catholic theological life. And there are countless publications in which we hear voices that startle us and make us exclaim: "Are there, after all, hopeful signs in the conflict between Rome and the Reformation?"

* * *

In the foregoing chapter we spoke about the new estimate of Luther. This development is interesting, but it does not affect the Roman church's ultimate conclusion that the Reformation was a revolution in the church in spite of all good intentions and religious ideas. However, the new theology, it seems, is concerned with deeper questions.

To the question of what constitutes the background of this noteworthy development, the answer is, I believe, that there is an undeniable, powerful influence coming from Biblical theology in this new theology. When the new theology called attention to the influence of (philosophical) forms of thought in a particular epoch, there was evident a tendency to go back of the scholastics to the Church Fathers, and back of the Church Fathers to Holy Scripture itself. There originated a new interest in the Bible, and even the Popes themselves issued a call to intensive Bible study.

For this reason it is necessary to observe the development of the new theology with great interest, not with exaggerated anticipations, which always disappoint, but with interest in the influence of the Word of God. When in the sixteenth century the Council of Trent accepted Scripture and tradition as of equal value as sources of revelation, Scripture at least remained accepted. And when, today, partly owing to the stimulus of Protestant Bible study, the Roman Catholic theologians again are fully occupied with the study of the Holy Scripture, then one must indeed be interested. For there is no one who can foretell the future. Rome itself may declare that the unchanging Roman church is the infallible authority, but a church which comes under the influence of the sovereign Word must begin to move. And for this reason we may not say that these developments are of no significance. We are living in times of tremendous tensions, scientific, philosophical, and especially religious. Everything is in motion.

We see this particularly in the latest developments in the Roman Catholic Church.

This question is now of extremely great significance: What is the judgment of the highest doctrinal authority regarding these developments? Has it been silent, has it rejected them or tolerated them? The answer to this question lies, for the time being, in the much discussed encyclical of 1950: *Humani Generis.*

CHAPTER FIVE

THE ENCYCLICAL *HUMANI GENERIS*

On August 12, 1950, the much discussed papal encyclical *Humani Generis* appeared. Regarded as one of the most important utterances of Pius XII, it concerns "some false opinions which threaten to undermine the foundations of Catholic doctrine." From this event it is quite apparent that the Pope sees dangers, and people naturally ask what dangers may be threatening now. The famous encyclical of 1907 was proclaimed when the danger of modernism threatened the church. The importance of *Humani Generis* is that it does not direct itself against errors outside of the Roman Catholic Church. Having cited certain errors, the Pope continues: "These and like errors, it is clear, have crept in among certain of our sons who are deceived by imprudent zeal for souls or by false science." There seems to be danger present in the church. And it is important to examine which dangers the Pope has in mind here.

*   *   *

When we analyze the encyclical we observe that the Pope warns first of all against conciliationism. The Pope perceives that many who see the dissension and confusion of humanity are consumed with a desire to remove the obstacles by which good and upright men are separated from one another. Thus people come to conciliation because they want to march together against the onrush of atheism. They want to come to a reform of theology and thus arrive at a more effective expansion of the kingdom of Christ over the entire world.

Now the Pope has no objections to a reforming, as such, of theology, provided that by this is meant an adaption to present-day circumstances and needs. "But some through enthusiasm for an imprudent 'eirenism' seem to consider as an obstacle to the restoration of fraternal union, things founded on the laws and principles given by Christ and likewise on institutions founded by Him, or which are the defense and support of the integrity of the faith . . . " And against this tendency the Pope warns with all his might, because it does not work for peace but for the subversion of what ever is essentially Catholic.

We observed in Chapter 3 that the Pope had already issued a warning in 1949. He now recalls this warning in *Humani Generis*. The explanation of this action is not that the Pope has no sympathy for peace, but that he sees within this conciliation an attack on holy matters, an attempt to make the church's authority relative. Particularly in small closed groups, so the Pope declares, people sometimes speak with a great deal of freedom. And "these opinions are disseminated not only among members of the clergy and in seminaries and religious institutions, but also among the laity, and especially among those who are engaged in teaching youth."

*   *   *

There is, however, much more against which the Pope directs himself in this encyclical. After conciliationism we may name, in the second place, existentialism. In order to make clear the dangers of the influences of existentialism, the Pope points out that at present the philosophy accepted and acknowledged in the church is being despised by some and referred to as old-fashioned. The philosophy of Thomas is attacked as being rationalistic. Over against this philosophy of unchangeable essentials is now placed the existence of individuals, and attention is called to the stream of events. The critics do not abandon Catholic dogma but they suppose that all sorts of philosophical conceptions are compatible with it. The Pope then specifically mentions existentialism, especially the kind that pays homage to atheism.

The Pope sees particular dangers in the underestimation of the intellect. He sees all kinds of irrational currents which make relative the ontological significance of reason. At stake is that which has been accepted by the church. In 1870 the Vatican Council maintained that God can be known with certainty by means of human reason, and before that the Borromeo encyclical had stated that God can be proved by human thinking. But now men are making reason relative and saying that it is insufficient for this knowledge and this proof. Men are calling into question man's entire being, not only the intellect, but particularly the feeling and intuition. According to the Pope it is plain that in this manner men arrive at ideas which are in conflict with the teachings of the church.

People are no longer interested in proofs for the existence of God; they regard such proof unnecessary. They prefer to demonstrate that the faith agrees with man's needs; they no longer wish to reach modern man by way of the bridge of human reason. "All these opinions and affirmations are openly contrary to the documents of our predecessors Leo XIII and Pius X, and cannot be reconciled with the decrees of the Vatican Council." The Pope then adds that one must pay heed to the doctrinal authority, which has the obligation to protect and explain the truth that has been revealed, and also to stand guard over scholarship. Thus the Pope cautions against irrationalism and sympathy for existentialism.

It has often been stated that the Pope rejects existentialism outright, for he couples it with atheism. But those among the Roman Catholics who seem to show some tendency to move in the direction of existentialism are not advocates of atheism at all. In 1948 by a decree from Rome the works of the atheistic existentialist Jean Paul Sartre were placed on the Index. All Roman Catholics whom the Pope is addressing in *Humani Generis,* accept this. Roman Catholic thinkers therefore point out that the Pope has no intention of rejecting all existentialism.

Thus after the issuance of *Humani Generis* we hear frank discussions regarding the significance of existentialism for Catholic philosophy, and it is said (for example, by J. B. Lotz) that this does not conflict with *Humani Generis* since the encyclical specifies only atheistic existentialism. The fact is that the encyclical is not clear. Moreover, it mentions no names, and consequently it is somewhat vague. From the encyclical it appears, however, that the Pope had more in mind than only atheistic existentialism. He warned against that type as the excess of existentialism. But those who have been influenced by existentialism cannot be called to order by *Humani Generis,* for, as they

maintain, they do not want to supplant the unchangeable
by the changeable, but to find a synthesis between the two.
Hence it cannot be gainsaid that the encyclical has failed to
solve the relation between existentialism and Catholicism.

*   *   *

Besides conciliationism and existentialism there is still
another important danger to which this encyclical calls
attention. This danger is frequently brought into direct
relation with the new theology. Again no names are
mentioned, but the expressions are nevertheless so selected
that certain names come to mind. The Pope's third
warning concerns erroneous ideas about dogma. The Pope
sees in the area of dogmatics, too, a grave danger from
relativism.

The beginning of this section reads: "In theology some
want to reduce to a minimum the meaning of dogmas;
and to free dogma itself from terminology long established
in the Church and from philosophical concepts held by
Catholic teachers, to bring about a return in the explanation of Catholic doctrine to the way of speaking used in
Holy Scripture and by the Fathers of the Church. They
cherish the hope that when dogma is stripped of the ele-
ments which they hold to be extrinsic to divine revelation,
it will compare advantageously with the dogmatic opinions
of those who are separated from the unity of the Church
and that in this way they will gradually arrive at a mutual
assimilation of Catholic dogmas with the tenets of the
dissidents." Obviously, dogmatic relativism is combined

here with conciliationism, but we are limiting ourselves now to relativism.

This section has, understandably, caused many people to look at the new theology, for this theology does indeed seek to return to the Fathers and to the Holy Scripture. Hence it is important to inquire more closely into what may be deduced from the *Humani Generis* encyclical with respect to the new theology.

We think particularly of the new theology when the Pope points out that theologians are saying nowadays that theology replaces old concepts with new, according to the modifications of thought in a particular time. "They add that the history of dogmas consists in the reporting of the various forms in which revealed truth has been clothed, forms that have succeeded one another in accordance with the different teachings and opinions that have arisen over the course of the centuries." According to the Pope, such thinking must lead to relativism in dogma. The danger exists that people will too readily adopt a new philosophy and that they will reject earlier formulations as being antiquated. The Pope stands up for the older formulations. Catholic believers from all ages have not simply used a specific, arbitrary philosophy, but have derived their concepts from a true knowledge of created things; and the church has strengthened them in this. Furthermore, some of the councils have even sanctioned some concepts in their conclusions, so that it is not lawful to deviate from them.

The Pope warns sternly: "Hence to neglect, or to reject, or to devalue so many and such great resources which have

been conceived, expressed and perfected so often by the
age-old work of men endowed with no common talent and
holiness, working under the vigilant supervision of the holy
magisterium and with the light and leadership of the Holy
Ghost in order to state the truths of the faith ever more
accurately, to do this so that these things may be replaced
by conjectural notions and by some formless and unstable
tenets of a new philosophy, tenets which, like the flowers
of the field, are in existence today and die tomorrow; this
is supreme imprudence and something that would make
dogma itself a reed shaken by the wind." Why should
one despise the scholastic theology which has been approved
by the church?

When Leo XIII issued his *Aeterni Patris* encyclical in
1879 he spoke of a restoration of Christian philosophy
according to the spirit of Thomas. On this point Pius XII
is certainly at one with his great predecessor. That is why
he is opposed to a return to Scripture and the Fathers,
not because they are not worthy, but because in this manner people seek to evade the emphasis of scholastic theology. Moreover, the Pope states that he is not simply warning against dangers; the new ideas "have already borne
their deadly fruits in almost all branches of theology."

It is not easy to know just what the Pope means by this
and whom he has in mind. For he speaks not only of the
doubt regarding reason (proof for the existence of God),
but also of the denial that the world had a beginning, the
uncertainty regarding the distinction between matter and
spirit, and other subjects. Finally he remarks: "Some even
say that the doctrine of transubstantiation, based on an

antiquated philosophic notion of substance, should be so
modified that the real presence of Christ in the Holy
Eucharist be reduced to a kind of symbolism . . . ." When
we take all these ideas together, we certainly cannot say
that they are exactly the ones which are advanced by the
new theology. No representative of the new theology has
advanced the above explanation of transubstantiation in
precisely that way.

And yet we cannot escape the impression that the Pope
seeks to issue a warning against the new theology, or
rather — for no names are mentioned — against certain
tendencies of that theology. These tendencies are: making
scholasticism relative, and consequently weakening the
ecclesiastical philosophy of Thomas. The Pope fears the
influence of relativistic modern thought. Although he
cannot deny that there has been a development of dogma,
he can only accept this development as a development from
the less clear to the more explicit, and he rejects the idea
that form and content can be separated. The church has
made its confession in the form and with the help of
Thomistic philosophical thought. Hence this form may
not be called relative, for that would do injustice to the
true character of dogma.

*   *   *

Nevertheless, the encyclical *Humani Generis* has not
produced a serious crisis. The well-known figures of the
new theology whom we mentioned have not been shunted
to the background. Instead, they are at the head of the
publicists. They are, indeed, concerned with the warning

of the Pope in *Humani Generis,* but their conclusion is
that they are not condemned by it.   Just as those who are
in sympathy with existentialism declare that this is not
in conflict with the encyclical, because the Pope has condemned only atheistic existentialism, so others say that the
Pope attacks only irrational misunderstanding of reason.
And they emphasize that they are in hearty agreement with
this attack.   Like the Pope they too acknowledge the peril
of irrationalism and agnosticism.   Thus, as far as I can
see, there have been no modifications in principle in the
publications of the new theology.

This is the peculiarity of the situation: on the one hand
the new theology is anxious to show that it is not in
conflict with *Humani Generis,* and on the other hand it is
captivated by the new questions, particularly in connection
with the evolution of dogma, so that it cannot let them
alone.

There are people who say that the new theology will
ultimately simply accept the church's doctrinal authority
as decisive and that therefore nothing will have changed.
In my opinion that is stating the problem too simply.
There appears to be a noteworthy development under way
in the new theology, which is closely connected with a
strong influence from Biblical theology.   Precisely here
lies the fascination of this theology.

In many respects scholasticism had succeeded in clouding
the outlook on Biblical truth.   When the Reformation
began in the sixteenth century it was precisely against
scholastic theology that there was emphatic objection.   Already in 1518 Luther composed a disputation against
scholastic theology, and with the liberation of theological

thought the Word of God once again had access to all
spheres of life. It is with the problem of the relationship
between scholasticism and the simplicity of the Gospel
that the new theology, too, is confronted. It is the same
problem with which Protestantism was confronted when
scholasticism came knocking on the doors of the church of
the Reformation.

That is why the new theology is such an important
phenomenon in present-day Roman Catholicism. When
there is a return in the church to the Word of God, nobody
knows what may happen. And this is the more true since
the new theology is not a new form of modernism. Modernism found fault with particular dogmas in the church,
but the new theology does not. A shifting is going on within the boundaries of the church. What the ultimate out-
come of this shift will be, one cannot foresee.

*   *   *

Whenever the church goes out into the world, it invariably meets new forms of thought. That is the problem
of the new theology. While the ecclesiastical authority
acknowledges the existence of development, it nevertheless seeks to keep this development very much along scholastic lines. But the new theology, while acknowledging
the infallibility of the church, has a greater appreciation
for the development of forms of thought; therefore it regards the utterances of the church as more historically
limited and looks for new formulation in a new age.

It is, from the Roman Catholic viewpoint, understandable
that the Pope is somewhat concerned, for church doctrine

manifests the aspects of scholastic forms of thought. And when men begin to tamper with these forms of thought, must this not eventually lead to a weakening of the dogma?

It is now seven years after *Humani Generis*. The movement of the new theology has not yet come to a halt. What will happen? Will the Pope be silent, or will he intervene once more and now more clearly than in 1950? We do not know. But there is reason to suppose that in the course of time there will have to be more clarity. The influence of the new theology is, I believe, increasing, although it meets with vehement opposition. Here we should recall the connection which the Pope makes between the new formulation of theology and conciliationism. He sees a connection, because making concepts of thought relative may lead to greater communion with those of a different persuasion. How is someone going to make a judgment on Luther when he himself has started to think critically about scholasticism and would be willing, for example, to accept much of Luther's criticism of 1518? Can the condemnation of the Reformation still be fully maintained?

It is of decisive importance for the development of the Roman Catholic Church how the ecclesiastical doctrinal authority eventually judges the new theology.

CHAPTER SIX

THE MOST RECENT PHASE

IN THE latest phase of the development of the new theology
Roman Catholic theologians are keeping themselves in-
tensively busy with the theology of Karl Barth and, by
way of Barth, with Reformed theology. As is well known,
Barth has been sharply disputing with Rome for more
than thirty years. As early as 1927 he attacked the Roman
doctrine of the church, and opposed particularly the so-
called natural theology, which was established in 1870 when
it was declared that man can know God simply with the
natural light of reason. In 1932, when Barth began his
Kirchliche Dogmatik, he wrote that he regarded the teaching of the analogy between divine and human existence
(as a ground for the proof of God's existence) as an inven-
tion of the Antichrist. He saw, in other words, a demonic
danger in it, because it assumes that man without grace
and outside of Jesus Christ is receptive to God and His
revelation. Barth emphatically denied this, maintaining
that no knowlege of God is possible outside of the revelation of God's grace. He attacked the Roman Catholic
contrast between nature and grace, and taught that grace
has precedence, as the basic design for creation too.

Barth's criticism of the Roman Catholic Church and

theology was so sharp that one scarcely expected to see early discussion or contact between Barth and Rome. But in 1951 one of the most brilliant adherents of the new theology, Hans Urs von Balthasar, wrote a detailed book regarding Barth — the two men know one another personally — in which he undertook to show that on the issue of natural theology at any rate there is no actual difference between Barth and Rome. Barth had misunderstood Rome at this point. The question with Rome was actually not a natural theology, but a Christocentric theology. In 1870 Rome had indeed formulated a "natural theology," but that was simply a defense against those who held human reason in contempt. (In my opinion this argument is a weakening of the entire structure of the Vatican Council, but we are now concerned with Von Balthasar's entire position.) On the issue of natural theology there is no good reason to permit the breach between Rome and the Reformation to continue. On this issue only, however, for there certainly is a profound difference between Rome and the Reformation regarding the doctrine of church and sacrament and regarding papal primacy. But that which Barth designates as the fundmental opposition can be disregarded.

Von Balthasar's book has evoked a great deal of discussion. It gives a profound analysis of Barth's development; and although it does not conclude with a conciliatory synthesis, it certainly voices a passionate call to conversation.

*   *   *

Since it appeared — and this is especially what we mean by the most recent phase — there has appeared a book which no longer treats the questions of Von Balthasar, but penetrates exhaustively into the doctrine of justification. We are referring to the voluminous book of Hans Küng on *Justification,* a discussion of the doctrine of justification as taught by Barth, in which he posits that there is no difference in principle between the doctrine of justification of the Roman Catholic Church and that of Karl Barth.

This position interests us particularly because the question is now that which has correctly been called the most central point of the Reformation: justification by faith alone. This development is the more interesting because Barth has continually attacked Rome's doctrine of justification. He has opposed *sola fide — sola gratia* (by faith and grace only) to the Roman Catholic synergism, in which man cooperates in attaining to a state of grace. And now comes Küng with the statement that Barth has been giving an incorrect interpretation to Roman Catholic doctrine, and that it was in fact Rome which was concerned with *sola fide — sola gratia.*

One can well understand that at the moment (Küng's book appeared in 1957) there is a great deal of stir about this remarkable book. What position the Roman doctrinal authority is taking with regard to this book, is not known. But with this authority in mind, it is important to examine whether Küng is indeed a pure exponent of the Roman Catholic doctrine of justification. Could it be true that *sola fide* is not specifically Reformed, but also Roman Catholic? Have we then been misinterpreting Rome all this while, or is Küng delivering an interpretation which cannot be maintained? And above all: if *sola fide —*

sola gratia is authentically Catholic, why then did the Council of Trent reject the Reformation's *sola fide* as heretical?

The questions that come up in connection with *sola fide* were of great importance in the time of the Reformation. People generally had the feeling that here was a decision of extremely far-reaching importance and that the entire controversy concentrated on this focal point. Does *sola fide* not imply a clearly drawn boundary which must be acknowledged by both sides? Does *sola fide* not function critically, just as do "only through Christ" and "only through the Holy Scriptures"?

It may be said that for many centuries the radical differences on this point have been generally acknowledged. Rome has always seen in the Reformation *sola fide* a one-sidedness. But now we hear in our own time Roman Catholic voices which state with emphasis that *sola fide* is not at all a specifically Reformation principle; Rome, too, confesses it. This development is related to the fact that Roman Catholic thinkers well understand that Paul's letters to the Romans and Galatians exerted an enormous influence on the Reformation, and that these letters are also in the Roman Catholic Bible, where they are regarded as the infallible Word of God. We need not be surprised therefore that these letters continue to speak in the Roman Catholic Church too, and that Paul's witness regarding faith and works can thus continue to exert its influence.

It is not true that Rome refuses to recognize these letters. On the contrary, it rejects the accusation of the Reformation that Rome disparages grace. People in the Roman Catholic Church also want to acknowledge grace, and they refuse to relinquish the confession of grace to the Reformation. And thus it has come about — specifically in our time — that we suddenly hear voices again which are speaking of the Roman Catholic *sola fide*.

Hans Küng is not the first to have spoken thus on the subject. In Holland, W. H. van der Pol, who left Protestantism and entered the Roman Catholic Church, has been teaching for years that at this point there is no actual difference. He writes, for instance: "Without any merit on the part of the believer his sins are forgiven him and the righteousness of Christ is granted him in exchange, strictly through grace alone. For if there were any mention here of merits, grace would no longer be grace." This, he maintains, is precisely the doctrine of the Roman Catholic Church. He writes further: "The *sola fide* as the Apostle Paul has in mind, particularly in his letters to the Romans and Galatians, is fully accepted by the Catholic Church." Others too declare that the Reformed explanation of the texts is correct, and that it is a misunderstanding to suppose that Rome does not profess the sovereignty of grace.

* * *

All this is discussed in great detail in Hans Küng's book. In the preface to the book Barth expresses his surprise regarding the manner in which Küng represents the Roman Catholic doctrine of justification, and he states that *if* this representation is correct, then — at least on this point — there is no longer any difference. There still remains enough to discuss, for instance, the primacy of the papacy, the sacraments (the mass!), and Mariology, but there is no longer any difference regarding *sola fide*.

Küng attempts to demonstrate that Barth, as well as others, has given an incorrect interpretation to Trent's formulation, and has made a synergistic doctrine of salvation out of it. Küng combats this with the greatest positiveness; his book contains two chapters entitled, "Sola Fide" and "Soli Deo Gloria." The time of antithesis, declares Küng, is past; an ecumenical contact, a new discussion, is in order. It is true that the (previous) utterances of the church are irrevocable and infallible, but it must not be forgotten that, for instance, the utterances of Trent were made in a polemical situation and were directed against heresy. One can therefore never learn to know true Catholicism fully from the pronouncements of such a council. In a defense there is always a certain one-sidedness, and the church in its defense suffers from this too. Küng speaks frankly about the limitedness of Trent. The accents simply had to be made in a one-sided manner.

According to Küng, once a person sees this he will realize that it has never been the intention of Rome to derogate in the least from the sovereignty of grace. It must be acknowledged, Küng says, that Holy Scripture is first of all concerned with the favor and grace of God, and with His sovereign mercy, and that theology has not done full justice to this nor has it always done justice to the teachings of Paul. But the Council of Trent was not concerned to deny the justification of the sinner. It simply sought to deny that the question in justification is merely a matter of *declaring* a person to be justified, of something external, in spite of which the person remains a sinner, a total sinner. When the Reformation asserted this, Rome was forced to answer, and accordingly the Council of Trent emphasized the change which justification brings about in a person. It was necessary to make apparent that something takes place in the justified sinner, that he is put to work, that he starts to cooperate. This does not mean that justification comes partly from God and partly from man himself, but simply that justification makes a person active. The Council did not wish to detract from Paul's word, "What hast thou that thou didst not receive?"

In answer to the question whether the meritoriousness of good works is not maintained by Rome or by the Council of Trent, Küng states that the meaning is simply the reward-concept of the New Testament, and he fully agrees with the word — which during the sixteenth century was constantly quoted by the Reformers against Rome — regarding the unprofitable servants in Luke 17:10: "So likewise ye, when ye shall have done all those things which are commanded you, say, We are unprofitable servants: we have done that which was our duty to do." He that glorieth, let him glory in the Lord!

Expressing his amazement in his preface to Küng's book, Barth states that he has been twice at the church of St. Maria Maggiore in Trent, but if Küng's representation of the teachings of Rome is correct, then he is willing to go to Trent once more with a confession of sin. But he first wants to see what the reactions of the official Roman church will be.

*   *   *

Meanwhile, it remains a question whether the decisions of the Council of Trent have indeed been interpreted incorrectly by us. It seems to me that it is precisely against *sola fide* that Trent turns, against the faith that directs itself exclusively upon the grace of Christ. The Council of Trent rejects the teaching that nothing more is necessary for the justification of the sinner than faith. True, it does cite a few texts from Romans, but at the same time it speaks of the disposition with which one prepares himself for justification. As early as 1520 Luther had been officially attacked and condemned on the grounds that he had denied the free will of man.

Is all of this a misunderstanding? We can scarcely believe it. Yes, indeed, says Küng, it is a misunderstanding: for Rome attacks the Reformation's external concept of justification. It is quite apparent, however, that the Reformation never entertained such an external concept. When the Council convened (1545) a great many Reformation confessions had already appeared and from these it was sufficiently clear that the Reformation *sola fide* did not mean that justification was merely an external matter which changed nothing at all within the sinner.

Both Luther and Calvin had contended with the Antinomians. Calvin at one time expressed it beautifully by saying that *sola fide* did not mean that faith remains alone. The entire Reformation approved what Lord's Day 24 of the Heidelberg Catechism declares: that the doctrine of justification does not make men careless and profane, "for it is impossible that those who are implanted into Christ by a true faith should not bring forth fruits of thankfulness."

Has Rome then misunderstood the Reformation? It is obvious that it has understood the Reformed doctrine of justification as being external, whereas the Reformation regarded justification and sanctification as inextricably related to one another. It is impossible to draw any other conclusion than that the declarations of the Council of Trent actually have reference to nothing but the Reformation *sola fide*.

*   *   *

This does not alter the fact, however, that the new voices which are heard at present are a witness to the power which the Word of God exerts, even in the midst of all kinds of fabrications of human thought. We do not mean to say that the controversy between Rome and the Reformation will now quickly become a thing of the past. But the Word of God is not bound, and time and again it breaks startlingly and with blessing from its fetters. Although we think that the Roman interpretation of Trent's wording is incorrect and historically untenable, and that more is signified by the meritoriousness of good works than the recompense in the New Testament, this does not alter the fact that Roman Catholic Biblical research — so heartily enjoined by the Popes — is not remaining unfruitful and that the Word in its clarity can make its power felt.

As is well known, every Roman Catholic is bound to accept the infallible doctrinal utterances of the church. No one is permitted to meddle with these. In our time, too, the decrees of the Council of Trent are generally accepted. The difference is simply this, that they are presently being interpreted in a manner in which people want to let *sola fide* be heard. This is an evidence of the crisis arising from Biblical thinking. And in the tensions of our time we wish to wait to see what the Word of God will do. For it is the Sword of the Spirit. It is quick and powerful and sharper than any two-edged sword, piercing even to the dividing asunder of soul and spirit and penetrating deeply into human life.

It is necessary first of all in this development that the Reformation faith is conscious of its riches and power, not out of a negative and barren anti-papism, but from a conviction of faith that the grace of God is sovereign and that the witness of *sola fide* was the power of the Reformation and that today it can still be the same.

CHAPTER SEVEN

THE POWER OF THE REFORMATION

———

WHEN WE SPEAK about the power of the Reformation, it may appear as though we stubbornly maintain something which actually seems to be quite contestable. Should we not rather speak of the *weakness* of the Reformation, both in its origin and in its continuation in later periods up until our own time? Is not this weakness still evident in all kinds of divisiveness and tension within the churches of the Reformation? Is there perhaps more reason to consider honestly the power of the Roman Catholic Church, which also experiences tensions and difficulties, threats and apostasy, but which nevertheless manifests itself in all kinds of ways in a powerful unfolding and influence?

It is not our intention to subject a variety of phenomena to a close scrutiny in order to compare Rome and the Reformation in respect to the actual unfolding of their resources. If that were our aim, we should have to note that the Reformation started in a small way and that this force often appears still to be small and inconsequential in comparison with the *Ecclesia Catholica* over the entire world.

*　　　*　　　*

When we speak about the power of the Reformation, we are concerned with the actual power. Wherein does

this power, this validity, reside? What was it that entered
into the hearts of thousands in that historic hour of the
church? In order to understand this properly, it is well
to look for a moment at the origin of the Reformation.
It has often been said that the Reformation originated in
Luther's psychological and moral tensions. It has been
supposed that he, utterly tormented and disturbed in
his inner self, finally loaded these tensions upon the
church's back and thereby precipitated the church into
the greatest possible confusion. This explanation of the
origin of the Reformation has been current for a long
time, in fact, right into our own century. Reformation
for the Roman Catholic dogmatist or historian has meant:
imbalance, disharmony, fragmentation, individualism, dis-
turbance of peace and unity.

That this explanation is altogether untenable becomes
increasingly apparent to anyone who observes how the
Reformation was growing in the years prior to 1517.
During this time there was discontent and criticism on the
part of many, but all of it failed to lead to a real Reformation. Why was it not Erasmus but Luther who became a
Reformer? The power of the Reformation is not to be
found in a certain imbalance and discontent and criticism.
With Luther it was a case of being bound more and more
by the Word of the gospel. Before 1517 Luther was
continually occupied with the Bible, with the Psalms and
with Romans and other parts of Scripture. He came into
new and vital contact with the Old and New Testaments.
That Word was previously in the church, but how ob-
scurely, and how complicated the way to salvation had
grown! When in the years before 1517 a new interest

and attention began to grow, something took place, just
as when the young Samuel said, "Speak, Lord, for thy
servant heareth."

The Word penetrates once more in a new and astonishing
manner and as a result everything stirs into action. The
Word begins to engross the hearts and lives of those who
are seized by it. It is not a question of theology, but of
listening and obeying, of trust and certainty, of going
through opened doors into a new land, the *old* land of
the gospel, of the gospel of the cross, which is the power of
God unto salvation to everyone that believeth.

It was not simply a question at the time of an abuse
here and a corruption there against which the Reformation
came into opposition. Luther knew perfectly well the imperfection of the church; and he did not issue a call to
revolt on perfectionist grounds. But he saw the gospel
in its power over the church. His witness of 1517 was not
intended as a breaking away from the church, but as a
mighty appeal of faith, a call to conversion and to repent-
ance. The reaction of Rome clearly showed that it did
not want to tolerate this knocking at the door, and that
too much was at stake. This is what led to the tremendous
conflict. Then Luther was threatened by papal excom-
munication and his books were burned in Louvain.

*   *   *

"Arise, O Lord!" — thus began the papal bull of June
15, 1520, which attacked the errors of Luther. Rome
realized that abuses had stolen into the church, and after
1520, by inaugurating a great variety of reforms, it en-

deavored continually to show that a reform could have
been possible within the Roman church under the direction of papal authority. But Luther and Calvin experienced that the mutilation of the gospel was not undone
and that in this respect the knocking at the door had
gone unheeded. Then the conflict came and it increased,
since the Roman Catholic Church did not want to hear
the doctrine and preaching of the Reformation.   The
conflict grew steadily more evident.   Over against the
Augsburg Confession of 1530 echoed the Roman "Nay!"
and when it had become clear what the Reformation
fundamentally meant, after 1545 the Council of Trent in
an irrevocable "Nay" made the breach definite. And its
anathema sit! ("cursed be") still thunders at us.

In this conflict it became unmistakably evident for all
future time wherein the strength of the Reformation lay.
Its force did not inhere in numbers, but in the truth, in
the gospel, in the Word of God, in listening anew to
the voice of God in the Bible, in rendering oneself captive
to the Word.   (The influence of the Reformation has been
incalculably great on the study of the Holy Scripture and
upon the preaching which is controlled by it.)   The light
of the gospel burst through in unprecedented strength.
All of life came into commotion and unrest. It was not a
revolutionary sentiment, but the renewed grasp for rest in
the Word which is for life and death, the renewed seeking
for the song of praise in the dogma of the church.

In this power the Reformation opposed, among other
things, the meritoriousness of good works, indulgences
and other abuses in the church which were symptoms of

the devaluation of the gospel, the strength and the authority and the hierarchy of the church. The clash that resulted was fearful. What courage of faith was required over against an honorable, and long, and all but undisturbed tradition! How they were suspected — these Reformers — of being nothing more than the representatives of a revolt of the masses! What had they started, and what would they be able to accomplish against this historic power! If they had allowed themselves to be guided by human considerations, they would certainly have capitulated — with and in spite of their objections — as Erasmus and so many others did. But they had been seized by the superior force of the gospel. Hence they stood, and they could not do otherwise.

They did not protest against the church, against good works, against authority, against office, but against the deterioration of all this. They fervently longed for the purity of the church and its preaching, for true authority, for works of gratitude, for the office of service. They again saw Jesus Christ as the Head of His Church, and they saw that there was and had to be responsibility in the church, a repeated call to order from the gospel. This was the focal point of their zeal, of their dogged tenacity. This was the strength of the Reformation. It was by no means a reaching for power — "No earthly power we do desire." The strength of the Reformation lay in the obedience of faith which liberated life for new, spontaneous service.

*　　　*　　　*

If anyone still wants to point out the weakness of the Reformers and the Reformation, he can write a whole book about it. Such books can always be written; in church history, too, it is true that "who glorieth, let him glory in the Lord!" The Reformers had their weaknesses, and imperfections marred their work. I have in mind the tension between Luther and Calvin, the fragmentation and division. Rediscovery of the new day came in the midst of imperfection and weakness. The breaking out of a centuries-old tradition and custom was anything but a simple matter. And if it had depended on people, nothing at all would have come of it. The weaknesses of the Reformation must be fully acknowledged.

But I think here of Calvin, who more than anyone else searched for the unity of the powers of the Reformation. The divisions frequently oppressed him, as did the tension with respect to Luther. But he looked beyond the weakness of human endeavor; even in the time of the tension with Luther he could distinguish: "Even though he should call me a devil, I should nevertheless regard him as a remarkable servant of God." The power of the Reformation did not lie in the nobility of human beings, but in the gospel itself.

In all weakness and imperfection the light shone through as the light of God. The Word penetrated once again and eyes became enlightened. Romans and Galatians and the Psalms were read and understood again, and people knew again the meaning of authority — more authority, more comforting authority, than Rome ever knew. People understood again that faith is not simply an intellectual regarding as true a number of truths, but that it is knowledge and trust, founded on the Word of promise. Preachers of the Word slashed away through every kind of uncertainty and despair and frustration in the life of faith, and they preached once more the only foundation that has been laid, which is Jesus Christ and Him crucified. His complete work became the source of a new life for comforted and thankful people. And they understood that we could not in a single respect have laid this foundation, but that it had been laid.

This is what gave the Reformation its power in interpreting the Bible, in preaching, in comforting and exhorting. This aroused a joy which was experienced as a gift, as a deliverance from all the stipulations of the involved penalty-doctrine and from conditions that first had to be met before one could taste the joy of the gospel. And in this manner, life — the full, ordinary life — was once more placed in the full light, in the light of the gospel. This was not a sentimental narrowing of the idea of God. It was precisely the Reformers who knew about the wrath of God, of God's judgment over sin, and who spoke about penalty, humility, and sorrow. But they understood what Psalm 90 teaches, that the light shines; in the flood of judgment and transitoriness it is possible to pray for the beauty of the Lord; we may rejoice and be glad all our days, and we may be satisfied early. The gospel stood again in the center. It remains one of the most shocking events of the sixteenth century that the Council of Trent hurled its *anathema* against *sola fide, sola gratia, sola Scriptura.*

*   *   *

It is a question for the future whether the churches of the Reformation still know and witness to what this *sola*

means. There have been times in the post-Reformation
era when people fell back into their own achievements,
when they undertook to live by their own inner light
and imagined that they no longer needed Scripture, when
they obscured the Word and sacrament, and when Protestantism degenerated into a hollow and barren protest
against restraint and authority. People then appealed to
"Protestantism," imagining that they saw therein simply
an awakening of the new, immense desire for freedom.
The Aufklärung is sometimes regarded as the consumma-
tion of this. With an appeal to Protestantism, critical
thinking came to stand in opposition to the gospel and
people began to anatomize the revelation of God, until
hardly anything of it was left. This Neo-protestantism
became the occasion for Rome to view the Reformation
in a critical light.

But this Neo-protestantism with its autonomy, its glorification of freedom, its criticism of Scripture and its
criticism of miracles is nothing but a caricature of the
Reformation. It has preserved nothing whatever of the
true power of the Reformation. It has profaned life and
robbed it of its subjection to the Word; it has made it
lonely and has isolated it, and in this manner has assisted
in the secularizing of life. This secularization has over-
whelmed man with problems of the individual and community, of authority and freedom, of dictatorship and
human sovereignty. In it tensions have piled up and
become insoluble, people have vaccilated back and forth,
and the powerlessness of life has become obvious.

This development is the result, not of the consequences,
but of the forsaking of the Reformation. For the strength

of the Reformation lay in the power of the Word. The
Reformation saw the power of the gospel; and this power
seizes all of life, The Reformation saw that religion is not
a fraction of life, side by side with other fractions, but
that all of life stands under the freedom of Christ and
in His service. For this reason the power of the Reformation made itself very actively felt in every area of life.
There was no turning away from the world, no anabaptistic
separation; rather, an acceptance of life in the service of the
obligations which God had given. To be sure, there was
a expectation of the future, of the return of Jesus Christ,
but this expectation did not weaken activity in the world;
instead it stimulated it. For the desire was to make the
service of God concrete. Life was made ready for this
service, in the proclamation of the gospel and in obedience
to the commandments, under the Divine rule which people
had now actually come to love. Life again had meaning
under the Word of Him whose kingdom was to come.

*   *   *

Thus the power of the Reformation has meaning for
all of life. When life threatens to become autonomous,
secularized and demoralized, when all comfort seems to
dissolve into a nihilistic and isolating view of life, when
life in the world appears to be more and more threatened
by a devaluation of God's command and of His glory —
precisely then the desire must burn in our hearts that the
power of the Reformation be manifested in our own lives.

In these times, amid the powerlessness of life, the Roman
church once again sends forth her invitation to seek

healing under her wings. Along the entire front between
Rome and the Reformation conflict over the truth has
again burst out fiercely. The extent of the conflict may be
measured by the flood of literature. And everyone feels
that it is not simply a theological conflict, but that all of
life is involved.

If we cannot do anything except protest a little against
authority and office, then we had better let October 31 slip
by unnoticed. If we do not love the church of Jesus
Christ and seek to promote its unity, then we shall never be
able to comprehend the controversy of the sixteenth century. If we no longer see the power of the Word and
scarcely read the Bible any longer, then our strength will
depart and we shall not be able to withstand the gathering
storm. But the gospel makes one free for service. We are
called to occupy our places and to be unafraid. No one
may let the comfort of his faith and his flaming zeal be
taken away because of statistical considerations.

Where is the healing power for the needs of these our
times? Are we going to regard percentages and let our
strength become paralyzed? Let no one forget that Luther
and Calvin, in times when humanly speaking there was
every occasion for despair, staked *all* their strength. In
this respect, too, let us be their disciples. Much has happened since then, but we can learn much from their faith,
their industry, their burning love, their attentive lives,
their service. In such love and in such service we are not
afraid, but we march forward. For the power of the Reformation was not the strength of man, but the strength
which manifested itself in weakness. "I can do all things,"
Paul once exclaimed, "through Christ which strengtheneth

me." That was the power of the Reformation.

How our own time needs people who stand in that power! The future is concealed; it rises out of the seeming chaos of the present. But from the aspect of the Reformation, the call to service is never as strong and penetrating as in times of chaos. In times when the challenge to steadfastness and light still resounds from uncertainty and gloom, we shall understand our call, the call to declare: "We know," not in self-exultation, but in thankfulness and in the consciousness of our responsibility to those who are wavering. In this consciousness we shall not simply protest — there are already too many ineffectual protests — but serve in the spirit of the Reformation and declare that joy and community for country and people, for society and education, for the nations of the world are to be found in the gospel of Him who still has all power in heaven and on earth.

More and more His rule is refused and Rome points us and our people to the completeness of His revelation in her church, which wants to encompass all of life. But we think of the struggle of the Reformation regarding true authority, the struggle which put an end to the ecclesiasticizing of life and placed it once again under God's rule and thus gave all of it certainty and blessing. And from this power the admonition goes forth which echoes the word of Isaiah: "To the law and to the testimony! if they speak not according to this word, surely there is no morning for them."

INDEXES

INDEX OF CHIEF SUBJECTS

INDEX OF PERSONS